STEPPING
INTO THE
BIBLE

STEPPING
INTO THE
BIBLE

Beverly E. Kostich

Illustrated by Ruth J. Sealy

Abingdon Press / Nashville

STEPPING INTO THE BIBLE

Library of Congress Cataloging-in-Publication Data

Kostich, B. E. (Beverly E.)
  Stepping into the Bible / B. E. Kostich.
    p. cm.
  Summary: Bible adventures in which the reader controls the plot.
  ISBN 0-687-40060-0 (pbk.   : alk. paper)
    1. Bible stories, English. [1. Bible stories. 2. Plot-your-own stories.] I.
  Title.
  BS551.2.K68   1988
  220.9′505—dc 19   87-34169
                                                                      CIP
                                                                      AC

Manufactured in the United States of America

You will want to READ THIS FIRST!

This is a very special book. It is special because it is your ADVENTURE into the Bible. Every adventure is one that you choose. Only you can decide WHAT HAPPENS NEXT in this story.

You will not be reading this book through page by page. At the end of each page you will have a choice or a decision to make. You will be the one who controls exactly what happens next! Whatever choice you make . . . whatever you want to see happen . . . turn to that page and start a whole new part of the adventure.

As you explore these TEN DIFFERENT Bible adventures, you will have an opportunity to meet some well-known Bible people. Just exactly who you meet and what story you experience is all up to you, because this is your book.

Now sit back, prepare for an exciting time, and have fun . . .

STEPPING INTO THE BIBLE!

STEPPING
INTO THE
BIBLE

You are a pretty normal boy. You live in an average sort of home. But every now and then, strange things happen in your life. For instance, only last week—remember?

"Time to get up!"

"Ommmmph."

"Get up this minute, or you'll miss church!"

"Uhhhh!" You peek one eye from under the covers. It is *so* early. The late movie on TV last night was too good to miss, but now you are *so* tired. Maybe you should just turn over and go back to sleep!

"Are you coming?" Dad's voice interrupts your sleepy thoughts. What are you going to do?

If you roll over and go back to sleep, turn to page 115
If you get up and go to church with your family, turn to page 10

You give your pillow one last hug and hit the floor. Still half asleep, you pull on your clothes and race down the stairs. Quickly, you grab a slice of jelly toast and stand munching by the garage door as Dad backs out the car.

Soon you arrive at church and realize that your fingers are sticky with jelly. You rub your hands together as you walk slowly down the steps to your classroom. Where is everyone? You can't ever remember its being so lonely and quiet. Usually the halls to the classrooms are alive with boys and girls at this time of the morning.

Suddenly the lights dim, flicker off, and come back on. Then the hall dissolves into mist. What's going on? As you grope your way forward, a narrow staircase rises out of sight to the left. Another rises into the mist to the right. Which set of steps do you take?

If you choose the left steps, turn to page 13
If you choose the right steps, turn to page 12
If you are afraid to move, turn to page 22

You step cautiously into the swirling mist of the steps on the right. Up two more steps and you can see nothing at all. But you step up once more, and the mist parts.

A bright sun is shining. Dry, sandy ground stretches out ahead of you. You see a crowd of men just over there. They are wearing the most unusual clothes—flowing robes! Some have tall shepherd's crooks over their arms. Others are carrying gifts. How strange!

As you start to step forward to look closer, you notice your own feet. Sandals! And what a silly striped robe you have on! You must catch up with someone to find out what is going on. Up ahead the men are separating into two groups. A group of shepherds begins making its way toward the dusty fields. Some of the men with gifts are talking together, murmuring excitedly. Which group do you join?

If you choose to catch up with the shepherds, turn to page 15
If you choose to join the men carrying gifts, turn to page 16

You step bravely toward the left steps. As you climb up and up, you feel the staircase wobble slightly. Then a sudden gust of wind blows all the mist away, and you look around in amazement.

Sandals are on your dusty feet. A coarse, striped robe covers your body, ending at your knees. As you tug on the bottom of the robe, you feel something brush against you. You jump three feet and turn to see a soft, cuddly lamb gazing up at you. Beyond it are many other sheep, spread out across a hillside.

You pick up a shepherd's crook from the grass and start across the field. When you walk, the sheep amble along behind you. When you stop to rest, they chew grass and wait with you. They seem to trust you and feel safe around you.

Suddenly, a loud roar splits the quiet! The sheep freeze in fear at the sound. A lion appears along the top of the hill. What should you do? Should you try to save the sheep by fighting the lion? Or should you run and save yourself?

If you choose to fight the lion, turn to page 17
If you choose to run, turn to page 18

The shepherds are talking excitedly as they walk. You catch up, and they share their news with you.

"We saw an angel!"

"We saw lots of angels!"

"They told of a baby being born. He is in Bethlehem. We are going to see Him."

You walk with the shepherds as they tell you about this baby. He is the Savior they have all been waiting for! The shepherds are hurrying so fast to get to Bethlehem that you have to rush to keep up.

"The angels sang the most beautiful—"

"They said if we went to the stable behind the big inn, we would find Him."

The shepherds are practically running by the time they come to the long, low cave where animals stay. The shepherds duck low to enter. Should you go in to see the new baby? Or are you so tired and thirsty that you stop first at the inn to get something to eat?

If you choose to follow the shepherds into the stable, turn to page 21
If you choose to stop and get a bite to eat, turn to page 23

You walk over to the circle of men who are carrying gifts. These wise men tell you about a star they have been following.

"It has led us all the way from far to the east of here."

"When the star appeared we knew a new king had been born."

"We bring gifts to give the new king. I have a bag of gold."

"He will like my gift. It is frankincense."

"I've got myrrh for the baby king."

The wise men climb onto their camels and invite you to join them. What a treat! As you ride along, you hear how they read the prophecy that one day God would send a special king to the people. They had seen the new star appear in the sky and had followed it for months and months.

"There it is! The star is over Bethlehem!" shouts one of them.

But you notice an inn. You can smell the food they are cooking there. You have not eaten for a long time. Should you stop and get some food, or follow the wise men to see if they find the baby?

If you choose to stop and eat, turn to page 23
If you choose to follow the wise men, turn to page 19

You can't desert the helpless sheep, you just can't! A new confidence fills you. It is a feeling you have never felt before. It is as if God were standing right behind you, giving you a special courage that can accomplish anything.

You look again to the tall grass where the lion is hiding. It pauses halfway down the hill, trying to decide which of the sheep to attack. The frightened animals draw close to you and bleat loudly. Your hand goes to your belt and closes over a slingshot. Should you try to hit the lion with a stone from your slingshot? Or do you dare to grab it with your bare hands?

If you decide to use the slingshot, turn to page 24
If you dare to use your bare hands, turn to page 26

You run faster and faster. The snarling of the lion makes you run harder than you have ever run before! You finally come to an old oak tree and scramble up it. Then you lie very quietly along a high branch. The lion comes sniffing along underneath. It walks around and around the tree. After what seems to be forever, it goes away.

Trembling, you slip down from the tree and look around. Dry, sandy desert stretches out in every direction. The land is bare except for a few nearby trees. There is a well in the middle of the trees. A bucket and a gourd stand by it. You get yourself a drink of water and wonder where you are.

Then, along the horizon, you see a string of camels. It's a caravan! Are you afraid of the people? Or do you wave to get their attention?

If you decide to wave to the caravan, turn to page 27
If you decide to hide until the caravan passes, turn to page 28

"Stop! Stop!" calls a soldier, as the wise men of the East begin leading you toward Bethlehem.

"King Herod, the king of all Judea, the representative of Emperor Augustus Caesar of Rome, demands your presence."

You and the wise men from the East are soon in Herod's palace. He is an old man, angry and mean-faced.

"This star you follow, to what does it lead you?" he demands.

One of the wise men answers him. "The star means a new king has been born. We follow it to worship him."

Herod grips his royal scepter and grits his yellowed teeth. "When you find this baby, come back and tell me. I too want to worship him."

The wise men nod and set off once again in their search for the baby who is to be a king. They follow the star back to Bethlehem, where it stops above a stable behind the largest inn on the town square. You have become very hungry and tired. Do you really want to see a little baby? Or would you rather go to the inn and rest and eat?

If you choose to go with the wise men, turn to page 21
If you choose to stop and eat, turn to page 23

You tiptoe into the quiet stable. A small baby is lying in one of the mangers. Sitting nearby you see a man and woman. They tell you their names are Joseph and Mary and they are from the city of Nazareth. They tell you that God spoke to them in a vision and told them they should call this baby "Jesus."

You reach out and feel the baby's soft, chubby hand. For just a second the tiny fingers curl around yours. Then the baby's eyes close in sleep.

"Such a beautiful baby!" you tell the family. Joseph tells you how he has come to Bethlehem because the king had ordered a census taken. Since Bethlehem is the birthplace of Joseph's people, this is where he had to bring his family.

You wonder what the future holds for this child. You walk out of the stable and look again at the nearby inn. The food smells so good. You decide to go eat that food you have been thinking about.

You do this by turning to page 23

As you stand there, not knowing what to do, the mist swirls up around your head. You put your hands up to wave some of the stuff away from your face.

"Hey, kid, stand there and hold this," a rough voice tells you.

"Huh?" The mist dissolves, and you find yourself on the edge of a large group of strangely dressed men. They are all wearing sandals and funny robes. Several follow the lead of the first man and begin taking off their outer cloaks. They hand them to you and go running off to join a shouting crowd.

While you watch, they begin grabbing rocks and throwing them at a young man in the center of the crowd.

You are afraid. Should you try to help the poor fellow being so mistreated? Or should you stand very still and hold the coats?

If you decide to help the fellow being stoned, turn to page 31
If you stand still and continue holding the coats, turn to page 32

You leave the others and enter the crowded inn. Soon you are settled at a table in the big hall. In front of you is a plate heaped high with food. It is so good to be out of the hot sun and to rest a bit. A soldier sits down at the same long table and smiles at you.

"I am on my way back to the palace to report to King Herod. Would you like a chariot ride into Jerusalem?"

That does sound interesting! Do you want to go with the soldier or just sit and rest? After all, this has been a very confusing morning.

If you choose to go with the soldier, turn to page 29
If you choose to rest a while, turn to page 30

You tighten your fingers around the slingshot. Slowly, so as not to provoke the lion, you bend down and pick up two small round stones. You fit one into your slingshot and whirl it around and around.

Thump! The stone zooms into the lion, hitting it over one eye. The huge beast staggers. You quickly fit the second stone into place and fling it at the dazed beast. Thump! It hits with terrible force. The lion sinks to the ground and is still.

The sheep begin eating again, and one small lamb nuzzles your knee. You pet the soft creature and comfort it by talking about what you did to the lion. Do you tell the lamb you are a pretty brave person, with great aim? Or do you explain that you seemed to feel God helping you?

If you did it all yourself, turn to page 114
If you feel God helped you, turn to page 37

A great feeling comes over you. You know that God will enable you to do anything! It so fills you that you lose all fear for yourself and leap past the frightened sheep.

You jump onto the lion's back. Your suddenly strong arms tighten around the animal's neck. The lion tries to turn its head to bite you, but your grip is too tight. The animal makes a low, growling noise and collapses under you. Then you stand up and push the lion to one side.

The sheep seem to know they are safe again. They start to feed on the nearby grass. You are very proud of what you have done. It makes you feel good to have saved the sheep. Do you think you became so strong only because the sheep needed you, or do you think God gave you this super strength for some additional purpose?

If God has a special plan for you, turn to page 39
If the sheep's needs are the reason for your strength, turn to page 114

The caravan comes much closer. You scramble down from the tree and wave to get its attention. Two of the men turn their camels aside and come to you.

"Oh, I'm so glad you stopped," you begin. "I saw a lion and—"

"Are you alone?" one of them asks.

"Yes, you see—"

The men laugh and look at each other. "We could make some extra money selling him in the slave market when we get to Egypt," one says to the other.

"I don't know, he is sort of scrawny. But I suppose he is worth something." And before you can say another word, your hands are tied and you are on a camel, bouncing off toward Egypt.

You are not the only one being sold. Another boy, a bit older than you, is riding a second camel. He tells you his name is Joseph.

"No talking," one of your guards calls out. The camel moves swiftly across the desert. Your mouth is dry and you are hot. Then your camel stumbles, and you start falling off one side. Are you able to hang on to the camel, or do you fall off into the desert sand?

If you manage to stay on the camel, turn to page 36

If you fall to the ground, turn to page 118

You stay in your tree and are very quiet as the caravan comes by. Some of the people stop for a drink at the well near you. As they talk, you find out they have some slaves to sell to the Egyptians. One of these is a boy a bit older than you. You are very glad you didn't wave.

When the caravan leaves, you start walking—in the opposite direction. After a while you come across some people from Syria sitting by the side of the road. One of the men is very sick. His name is Naaman. He tells you he is on his way to visit a man who may be able to cure him. Naaman invites you to travel along with him. What do you do?

If you join Naaman on his trip, turn to page 38
If you continue on your own way, turn to page 45

"Oh, yes, I'd like to go to Herod's palace," you reply to the soldier.

"Then finish eating and let's get started." He grins as he throws some coins on the table.

Soon you are standing beside the tall, broad-shouldered Roman soldier in a sleek, shiny chariot. The horses snort and stamp. Then the soldier hands you the reins, and you snap them across the horses' backs. You race down the road at a dizzying speed. What fun!

When you get to the palace, you follow the soldier as he reports to King Herod. "People are talking of a child that has been born. They say He is to be some kind of a Savior."

The king screams out, "I want this child killed—*killed!* Do you hear me?"

"But we haven't found the baby! We don't know which child it is," answers the soldier. "We don't even know exactly how old He is."

"Then kill them all! All the children under two years old!"

The soldier marches out, with you close behind. Do you try to get back to Bethlehem and warn the people of what is to happen?

If you stay with the soldier, turn to page 34
If you try to warn the people in Bethlehem, turn to page 35

You watch the soldier leave, then sit back to relax. Your head begins to nod.

"Hey you, kid," a loud voice wakes you. "Are you going to pay for that food?"

You see that the other diners have gone their way while you napped.

"Well, kid, are you trying to cheat me or something?" A large, rough-looking man stands over you.

"No problem," you tell him, and begin searching for some coins. Only you can't find any. As you hunt for your money, he grabs your arm and begins shaking it.

"No, no!" You try to pull your arm free.

"I was only waking you up," says your best friend, Chuck.

You look around and see that you are standing near your Sunday school classroom. Chuck smiles at you and points to your hand.

"I see you are all ready for today's missionary offering."

You look down at the coins in your hand.

"Huh? Well, I guess that must be what they're for." As you talk, you brush bread crumbs from your shirt—*bread crumbs?*

The End

You drop the coats and push your way through the crowd of people. A man picks up a rock to throw, and you grab his arm. Someone else pushes you aside, and a stone smacks into your arm.

"That hurts," you yell. Another rock comes sailing through the air and hits you on the knee. "Ouch!" You are close enough to see the young man now. The men call him Stephen. His face looks like the face of an angel. He does not fight back as the stones hit him again and again. You are so close that many of the rocks that miss him thud into you.

You see Stephen kneel down and lift his face up toward heaven. Then a rock hits his beautiful face. Many others follow. Soon Stephen is buried under the rain of rocks. You get several bruises from stones that miss him. You slip back through the crowd, very frightened. You really don't understand why the people are so angry.

After you go a long way, a man in a rough robe stops you and asks if you are hurt. Do you ask the man why the people stoned Stephen?

If you ask about Stephen, turn to page 44
If you hurry away before you get into trouble, turn to page 119

Coats pile up around you as you watch the shouting people. The young man in the middle of the group is named Stephen. He is telling of God's goodness to His people and how they have not always done His will.

This is not very pleasant to hear! You understand why the people are angry. They attack this young man who has such strong ideas.

Stones fly through the air. You watch as one lands on his shoulder. Then he is hit on the head. Instead of yelling, the young man's face looks calm and peaceful. As the rocks continue to rain down on him, Stephen looks toward heaven and with a beautiful smile on his face says, "I see the heavens opened, and the Son of Man standing on the right hand of God."

This really makes the people angry. Soon rocks are falling on him from every direction. Stephen speaks a few more words and then falls flat on the ground, badly hurt. More stones are thrown. You watch as Stephen dies. People like him are troublemakers! Do you decide to go to work to help get rid of all those who feel as he does? Or do you walk away?

If you choose to rid the world of such troublemakers, turn to page 40
If you choose to walk away, turn to page 41

You decide it would be useless to try to find your way to Bethlehem on your own. You go with the Roman soldier as he gathers up his troops and then ride in his chariot with him as they return to Bethlehem. When you get there, the soldiers carry out King Herod's orders.

You watch in horror as they begin killing all the small children. Parents are crying and wailing in grief. It is so sad. You wonder how anyone could be so mean as to order a thing like this.

The soldiers prepare to return to the king to report on their mission. You may ride back in the big chariot if you want. What do you decide to do?

If you stay there in Bethlehem, turn to page 42
If you ride back to hear the soldiers report, turn to page 58

This is terrible! The people in Bethlehem need to be warned. You start running down the road. In a few minutes the king's soldiers come racing past in their chariots. You are left standing in a cloud of dust. You are too late! Nothing can save the little children now.

Discouraged, you sit down in the dust. You are so sad. You feel like crying when you think of all those tiny children . . .

"Hey, why so sad?"

You look up and see your best friend standing beside you in the hall outside your Sunday school classroom.

"I was thinking about—it's hard to explain," you sigh.

"Well, come on, we will be late for class."

You start to follow, then, from very far off, you think you can hear the sound of the soldiers' galloping horses again. No, you think, that can't be. You rush off to your classroom. Your lesson today is supposed to be about Jesus' birth and early years.

The End

You fling your tied hands out and grab the hair of the camel's neck. You manage not to fall off.

Finally the caravan stops to rest for the night. As you sit around the evening campfire, Joseph tells a strange story.

"Once, a long time ago, I dreamed that eleven stars, the moon, and the sun all bowed down before me. When I told my family about it, they seemed to think it meant I wanted to rule over them one day. My brothers became very jealous. I am here because they sold me to these people to get rid of me."

This is some strange story Joseph is telling. You wonder if he is making it all up to impress you, or if it really happened. What do you decide?

If you believe Joseph, turn to page 47
If you do not believe Joseph, turn to page 50

You run your fingers through the lamb's soft, fuzzy wool and try to understand what happened to you. It was as if God was right beside you, guiding your arm the entire time. You continue caring for the sheep and wonder what God has in store for you next. Then a messenger calls you to come with him to a feast. When you arrive, a man named Jesse says he is your father.

"Come, David," he tells you, "we have a visitor." Your father introduces you to a man named Samuel.

Samuel looks at you very closely. Then he stands up and does a strange thing. He takes some oil and pours it on your head. Everyone watches. You wonder what this could mean. Then you are sent back to the fields to watch your sheep.

Since you are all by yourself, you decide to keep busy with a hobby. How do you spend your time?

If you practice with your slingshot, turn to page 56
If you learn to play the harp, turn to page 60
If you write poetry and songs, turn to page 62

As you travel, Naaman tells you about himself. He is a captain in the army of Syria. He is a good soldier and an important man. But he is very sick with leprosy, a disease for which the doctors have no cure.

When he was in his own land, he and his king heard that a prophet in the land of Israel could cure leprosy. Naaman is on his way to search for this man. He is carrying a great bag of money and many new clothes as payment for his cure.

You accompany Naaman on his trip, being careful not to get too close to him. After all, you don't want to catch his leprosy. When you have gone a long way you arrive at the home of the great prophet Elisha.

Naaman waits at the door. Will Elisha answer the door and talk to this stranger in his land? What do you think?

If you think Elisha will come to the door, turn to page 78
If you think Elisha will send a servant, turn to page 46

You know there must be something very special in store for you, for God to give you such strength. While you ponder, a lady sits down beside you.

"You have been a special son to me, Samson."

You look around. She is talking to *you!*

"God has great plans for you. Our people have been mistreated by the evil Philistines for too long a time. Somehow, I know God will use you to free us."

You can hardly wait to hear what else she has to say!

"God will use you, but you must promise to do some special things. God expects you to keep your Nazirite vows. That means you may never drink strong drink or wine, and you must never cut your hair."

"My hair?" you answer. Surely this is a strange vow. Will you promise to try to keep this Nazirite vow? Or do you think the idea is silly? What do you decide to do?

If you promise to accept the vow, turn to page 48
If you laugh and leave this place, turn to page 111

You are very upset because many people have the same ideas that Stephen had. They do not want to worship God the way your people have always done. They have heard of someone called Jesus and believe He is some kind of a Messiah or Savior. Even though Jesus was killed, these people claim He lived again after only three days.

You go to the synagogue, and the priests there give you official papers that allow you to arrest those who do not worship in the old ways.

You work very hard. Many people are beaten, others are put into prison. Because you persecute these Jesus followers, they leave the city and scatter themselves across the countryside. You hear that some of them are in the city of Damascus. You consider going after them and bringing them back to be punished. What do you decide to do?

If you stay in Jerusalem, turn to page 61
If you go to Damascus, turn to page 57

You turn from the pile of stones that are heaped high over Stephen's body. It is difficult for you to understand how anyone could die with such a peaceful look on his face.

As you wonder, a strong wind begins whipping dust up into your eyes. You reach up to brush the sand and grit from your face. The wind blows so hard you cannot see.

When you can finally see again, you are standing on the hall steps near your Sunday school classroom. At the landing you see two narrow sets of steps. They seem to quiver, and then you see only the wide steps to your classroom again.

In class, your Sunday school teacher begins talking about a young man named Stephen. You hear how his great faith in God gave him courage to handle death without fear. You feel you can see exactly how his face looked when he gazed up into heaven and saw his Lord.

You know you couldn't have really seen his face. You brush some strange sand and dirt from your shirt. No, it couldn't be—could it?

The End

You decide you have seen enough Roman soldiers for a while, and so you say good-bye. You walk sadly down the street, wondering if the king's soldiers were able to find the baby the king was so worried about. You hope that the baby got away somehow.

You are getting tired, but you walk on and on, into the hills of Judea. Finally, completely tired out, you come to a small house. The kind man and his wife you meet there take you in and feed you.

Zechariah and Elizabeth are very old. They are caring for a young child. You ask if it is their grandson. Elizabeth smiles and tells you an unusual story.

"My husband and I always wanted a child, but we never had one. We prayed about it all the time. Then one day a wonderful thing happened."

What she tells you next is hard to believe. Could John really be their own child? Or do you believe they found him on their doorstep?

If you think John is their own child, turn to page 73
If you think they found John, turn to page 108

You tell the man about Stephen and all that happened. "What," you ask, "made everyone so angry with Stephen?" You are still upset by all the violence, and sore from the few stones that hit you.

"Well," the man in the robe answers you, "Stephen was reminding the people how good God had been to them, and how they have not always done His will. This upset them a lot."

"That's all he did?"

"Stephen was a follower of Jesus. Have you heard of Him? He was sent from God to save the people from their sins. But not many of these people believe that. They killed Stephen to shut him up." The man gathers his rough robe about himself and starts to leave. "What about you? Are you a follower of this Jesus?"

Several strangers are standing around. You wonder if any of them are men from the group that stoned Stephen. You don't want stones thrown at you. What do you say?

If you deny following Jesus, turn to page 64
If you admit that you follow Jesus, turn to page 112

Ugh! You do not want to travel with a sick man. So you watch the Syrians ride off and continue walking.

The way is hot and dry. You begin to wish you had gone with Naaman, or stayed by the cool water at the oasis. Then, when you are so thirsty you can hardly stand it, you see people and camels up ahead. This time you wave and yell.

Three men are leading a string of pack camels across the desert. They stop to see what you want.

"I'm lost. I'm thirsty. Will you give me some water?" you plead.

"Are you all alone?" one man asks you.

"Yes. Please help me."

The three men exchange glances and laugh. "I think we've found a slave to sell at the market in Egypt."

"No, no!" you say. But they just laugh harder, tie your hands, and dump you across a camel. They hurry the camels to a gallop to make up for lost time. You begin to slip off your camel.

Try to keep from falling and turn to page 118

When the door finally opens, it is Elisha's servant who speaks to Naaman. He doesn't ask what Naaman wants but gives him a message from the prophet Elisha.

"You are to go to the Jordan River. When you get there, wash yourself, all over, in the river. Then wash again and again. When you have done this seven times, you will be healed."

Naaman is very angry! He expected Elisha to come out and touch his leprosy and so heal him. Naaman begins to yell.

"I didn't come all these miles to take a bath in a river. There are better rivers at home than the dumb old river Jordan you have here!" And Naaman stomps off.

You run after him. "Mr. Naaman," you call.

"What now?" he says, turning to you.

"If the prophet had asked you to do something very difficult, would you do it?"

"Of course. This sickness is awful."

"Then why be angry because he suggests something easy? Why don't you try it?" Have you convinced Naaman to bathe in the river?

If you have convinced Naaman, turn to page 51
If you have not convinced Naaman, turn to page 52

As strange as his story is, you believe it anyway. You fall asleep wondering about him. Early the next morning, you are both put on camels, and the journey continues. After a very long time you see some buildings ahead. It is the capital city of Egypt. The traders sell Joseph to an army officer named Potiphar.

Potiphar looks at you. "Who is this scrawny-looking kid? He sure isn't worth much."

"We will sell him real cheap," the trader says.

"I don't know," Potiphar answers. "What about it, kid. Will you work hard for me?"

There are lots of other slave buyers around. You can hope someone nicer buys you, or you can promise the army officer you will work hard, and stay with Joseph. What do you do?

If you promise to work hard, turn to page 49
If you hope someone else buys you, turn to page 53

You promise to do what God expects of you. Never will you take strong drink, wine, or have your hair cut. You grow up into a fine, strong young man.

You use your great strength to help free your people from the cruel Philistines. Then you fall in love with a beautiful Philistine girl. She begs you to tell her how you got to be so strong.

"If you really loved me, you would tell me," Delilah pleads.

"It is a secret," you explain. "I cannot tell even you."

"Please, Samson. Pretty please."

After a long time and much begging, you finally tell her that you must never have your hair cut.

"Oh, Samson, I'm so glad you trusted me with your secret," Delilah thanks you.

As soon as you fall asleep, Delilah and her Philistine friends cut off all your hair. When you wake up, you feel your head.

"What have you done?" you roar. They all laugh and tie you up. You are too weak to break loose. Your great strength is gone. Someone suggests that they put out your eyes. Would they really do such a terrible thing? What do you think will happen?

If you are taken off to jail, turn to page 67
If your eyes are poked out, then you are taken to jail, turn to page 69

Since Joseph is the only person you know in all of Egypt, you promise Potiphar that you will do your best for him. He tosses a couple of coins to the traders and takes the two of you to his home.

Potiphar and his wife treat the two of you kindly. Joseph becomes a favorite of the army officer, and after a while is running much of the household for him. Potiphar's wife is kind to both of you for a time. Then she tries to get Joseph into trouble. When this doesn't work, she tells her husband lies about him. Potiphar believes her and is so angry he has Joseph put in prison. Do you try to explain the truth to the army officer, or do you keep quiet and try to stay out of trouble?

If you decide to keep quiet, turn to page 110
If you decide to defend Joseph, turn to page 55

"Come on, Joseph, that can't be true," you tell him.

"I had another dream, too," he adds. "I was working in a field with my family. We were all binding sheaves of grain. My sheaf stood up and everyone else's sheaf bowed down to mine."

"How exciting!"

"That's not what my brothers said about my dream."

"Were they angry? Did they think they would have to bow down to you someday? Is that why they sold you to these traders?"

"I don't know what they thought, but I know they didn't like me. Except maybe my brother Reuben. Sometimes he was nice to me—Well, he was nicer than the others, anyway."

"That is a very strange story," you tell him.

A guard begins talking to Joseph. This is your chance! While the guard is not watching, you can run away. Do you leave your new friend, Joseph? Or do you stay and see what happens next to this remarkable young man?

If you run off across the desert, turn to page 118
If you roll over and go to sleep, turn to page 47

You don't want to be an army officer's slave. You watch as Potiphar takes Joseph off to his home.

"Ouch!" You jump as someone grabs your arm. You look up at a huge fat man. He grins and shakes you.

"How much for this undersized piece of trash?" he asks the traders.

"Not much; we know he's not good for much."

The big man tosses them a coin. "This should cover what he is worth." Everyone laughs as he drags you away. The man takes you to an old ship and pushes you down below the deck.

"Bail, kid, bail," the man bellows.

You begin bailing smelly, slimy water. Soon your hands are sticky and dirty. The man shouts for you to bail faster. You work for hours.

"Speed it up."

You look up and see your best friend. "Speed it up, buddy. You're blocking the way. We need to get into our Sunday school classroom."

"Yes, sure," you answer. You are glad to sit down and rest. You feel like you still have slime on your hands; you look down and see jelly on your fingers. You laugh and sit back to enjoy your lesson.

The End

You try to convince Potiphar that Joseph is not guilty of doing anything wrong.

"If you think he is so great, you can go to prison with him," Potiphar shouts. You are sent off to jail. After a while, Joseph's talent for running things is noticed by the keeper of the prison. Joseph helps oversee the jail.

One day as you follow Joseph on his rounds, two prisoners tell Joseph about their strange dreams.

The first man, a butler, explains, "I saw a grapevine. In my dream I made juice from the grapes and gave it to the Pharaoh to drink."

The second man, a baker, speaks next. "I saw three baskets of food balanced on my head. I was taking them to the Pharaoh, but some birds came and ate all the food."

When they are finished, Joseph looks to you. "Which dream do you want me to explain?" he asks.

If you choose the baker's dream, turn to page 68
If you choose the butler's dream, turn to page 72

Your slingshot is in your hands all the time. You practice hitting targets farther and farther away. Soon you can sling a stone with super-special accuracy, and with great force.

One day Jesse sends for you again. "I want you to carry some food to your older brothers who are serving in King Saul's army. They are meeting the army of the Philistines at the valley of Elah."

"Yes, father," you reply. You arrive just in time to hear a challenge issued by a Philistine giant named Goliath.

"I defy the armies of Israel. Who dares fight me?"

All the soldiers are afraid. Goliath is half again as tall as the tallest man. He is covered with heavy armor and is waving a huge spear.

"I will fight Goliath!" you exclaim. "I believe the living God of Israel will help me." You step out with only your trusty slingshot, five stones in a small pouch, and God in your heart.

Goliath comes at you! You slip a stone into your slingshot. Where do you aim? You sling your stone toward what part of Goliath?

If you aim at Goliath's forehead, turn to page 70
If you aim at Goliath's heart, turn to page 76

"I will arrest every follower of Jesus I can find," you mutter as you travel to Damascus with some friends. Suddenly, a bright light shines from heaven. You fall to the ground as a voice speaks.

"Why do you persecute me?"

"Who are you, Lord?" you ask.

"I am Jesus, whom you are persecuting."

Very afraid, you ask, "What do you want me to do?"

"Go on to Damascus. You will find out there."

You start to get up. "I can't see! I'm blind! Help!"

"I'll lead you," one of your friends says.

You take the man's hand and stumble on to the city. For three days you are blind. You are too upset to eat or drink. Finally God sends a man named Ananias to you. He touches you and says, "Jesus sent me."

"I can see!" you shout. "Please, Ananias, baptize me. Then we will eat and you and your friends can tell me more about Jesus." You have been so cruel to the followers of Jesus; will they trust you now?

If they welcome you to their ranks, turn to page 91
If they think you are trying to trick them, turn to page 84

Once again the soldier lets you hold the reins. You slap them against the horses' flanks to make them go fast. The soldier laughs and encourages you to make the chariot race even more rapidly. At a sharp bend in the dirt road the wheels begin to slip on the rough dirt. The chariot slides to the edge of a steep cliff. You grip the reins so tightly that they bite into your palms, raising red welts. One wheel hangs over the edge.

"What do I do?" you scream. The soldier grabs for the reins, but the other wheel of the chariot drifts off the road, and you turn over and over. Down and down you fall.

It is so far. You see the steps down, down below you. Steps? You hold tight to the railing and look around at the familiar staircase leading to your Sunday school classroom. For just a second there you felt like you were falling. Strange thoughts had flashed through your head—something about babies crying and a racing chariot. How silly.

You notice red welts across your palms. You must have been holding onto that stair railing really hard—what else could it be?

The End

You often play a harp for the sheep. It seems to calm them on stormy evenings. You become a very skillful player.

Then one day your father, Jesse, sends you to take some gifts to King Saul. The king is impressed with you, particularly with your skill on the harp.

"Why don't you stay with me and be my armor bearer?" Saul asks you.

"If my father will let me, I would like that," you answer. And so you come to live in the palace. One day Saul is very upset. He is so angry that everyone in the palace is afraid.

"Perhaps you could play your harp for him," a servant suggests.

"I'll try," you answer. Soon the sweet sounds of your playing fill the palace, and Saul becomes calm again. After that, whenever he has one of his angry spells, you soothe him with your music.

One day a messenger tells Saul that the army of the Philistines is massing for battle. This means war! You are considered too young to be a soldier, so are sent back to care for your father's sheep.

You do this on page 56

"I have hunted enough Jesus-followers. It is too difficult a task," you tell your friends.

Because you do not chase them, the followers of Jesus return to Jerusalem and form a small church. They have no need to leave their city, so the gospel is not carried across the world.

In later years, this small church is unknown outside the immediate area of Jerusalem. Thousands never hear that He came to earth to redeem them from sin, because you did not make this small church scatter and take the good news of Jesus' love to all the world.

"No! No! It's not my fault!"

"What are you talking about?" your Sunday school teacher asks.

You look around and see you are standing in the hall outside your classroom.

"Come on," your teacher says, "time for class. Today we will be studying about the persecution of the early church in Jerusalem."

"And this time, I'll make them scatter. I'll chase them and—"

Your teacher looks at you and shakes his head. You smile. He just doesn't understand. But you do.

The End

You take good care of the sheep and help pass the time by writing poems and songs. You sing some of the songs to the sheep and play music on your harp, too. It is a restful, sleepy time.

"Hey, are you going to stand there all day?" asks Chuck, your best friend.

"Huh?" you answer. You look around and find yourself in your Sunday school classroom.

Your teacher begins today's lesson by telling the class about the life of David.

"The prophet Samuel anointed him to be king when he was very young. Later he played his harp for King Saul, fought Goliath with a slingshot, and one day became king." Your teacher asks, "Does anyone have any questions about David?"

"I thought David wrote poetry and sang songs," you say.

"You're right. David wrote some beautiful poems and songs. Many of them can be found in the Bible in the book of Psalms."

"How did you know that?" Chuck whispers to you. You look at what appears to be lamb's wool on your sleeve and tell him it would be hard to explain.

The End

Naaman shivers in his blanket. Then he slowly uncovers an arm. There are no white patches on it. None on the other arm, either. Naaman drops the blanket and looks at his body. All the swollen white patches are gone! Naaman is cured! You both are very excited and happy. Naaman dresses, and the two of you hurry back to the prophet's house.

Elisha is waiting. Naaman rushes up to him and speaks. "I know now that the only true God is the God that you serve. I want to thank you for asking Him to heal me. I have brought you a great treasure to thank you." Naaman points to a bag of silver and to a pile of new clothes.

Elisha says he cannot accept the gifts. Naaman looks at you for help in deciding what to do. Do you tell him to insist that Elisha take the treasure? Or do you tell him to do as the prophet wishes?

If you say to insist, turn to page 65
If you say to do as Elisha says, turn to page 66

"No, not me. I'm not even from around here. I don't know anything about J—"

"Don't worry, I understand," the man tells you. "Why don't you walk along with me for a while?"

"I'd like that," you answer. Something about this man makes you feel safe. After the two of you have left the others behind, the man stops at a small stream to rest.

"My name is Peter," he begins. "I knew Jesus very well. I traveled with Him, and I was there when He was arrested."

"What did you do?"

"After they arrested Jesus, I was afraid the same thing might happen to me. Three different people asked me if I knew him. Each time I said I didn't." Peter pauses and looks very sad. Then he pats you on the shoulder and goes on. "So you see, I know exactly how you must be feeling right now."

Your face turns bright red.

"Come," Peter tells you. "I will show you where Jesus died." Do you want to go with Peter?

If you say yes, turn to page 71
If you say no, turn to page 120

You tell Naaman you think he should insist that the prophet take something for healing him. Naaman tries again to give the treasure to Elisha. Elisha refuses to accept anything.

Naaman is so impressed that he tells Elisha, "I will never again give an offering or make sacrifices to the gods of the land where I live. I will only respect the one true God, the one that gave you the power to heal me."

Elisha answers him, "Go in peace."

And so Naaman begins his trip home. As you all travel down the road, you see Elisha's servant, Gehazi, running after you. He tells Naaman that his master has changed his mind and wants part of the payment that was offered to him.

Naaman happily gives Gehazi even more than he asks for. You wonder about this change of heart and decide to say good-bye to Naaman and follow Gehazi.

Follow him to page 79

66

You tell Naaman he should do as the prophet wishes. Naaman thinks about your advice, but decides to insist anyway. He tries again to get Elisha to take the treasure he has brought. Elisha refuses to accept anything.

Naaman is so impressed that he tells Elisha, "I will never again give offerings or make sacrifices to the gods of the land where I live. I will only respect the one true God, the one that gave you the power to heal me."

Elisha answers him, "Go in peace."

And so Naaman begins his trip home. As you all travel down the road, you see Elisha's servant, Gehazi, running after you. He tells Naaman that his master has changed his mind and wants part of the payment that was offered to him. Naaman happily gives Gehazi more than he asks for.

You wonder about this change of heart and decide to say good-bye to Naaman and follow Gehazi.

Follow him to page 79

Even the terrible Philistines wouldn't put your eyes out. No one could be that cruel!

But you are wrong. They poke out your eyes and hitch you to a grinding wheel in the prison. Day after day you walk around and around, grinding grain for the evil Philistines.

Still, they are not satisfied. A great holiday is approaching. It is a celebration of the fish-god, Dagon. The Philistines decide to bring you to Dagon's temple to make fun of you. They don't notice how much your hair has grown during your months in prison.

At the temple, you hear the jeers and screams of the celebrating people.

"I am tired," you tell the lad who is leading you around. "Let me lean against the big pillars that hold up the building. I need to rest."

He snickers at your weakness but places your left hand on one pillar and your right hand on another. "There, Samson, you rest here in the middle of the temple where everyone can see what a pitiful sight you are." He laughs as you bow your head. Your new long hair falls around your face as you pray.

Turn to page 116

"Well," Joseph explains, "the three baskets stand for days. In three days Pharaoh will have you taken out of prison and hung. Your body will be left out so that the birds may come and pick it to pieces."

"Awk!" the baker gags; he runs back to his cell in fear.

Three days later the guards come and take him away. From your cell window you watch the birds circle around his body.

"Joseph," you ask, "how were you able to figure out what the dream meant?"

"I didn't," he tells you. "Interpretations belong to God. He revealed the dream to me."

"Did He reveal the meaning of the butler's dream, too?"

"Yes," Joseph answers. Both you and the butler look expectantly at him.

He explains on page 72

"Aaaaaaaaaaah!" you scream. The terrible Philistines have poked out both of your eyes. Blind, you are tied and dragged off to jail. They hitch you to a grinding wheel in the prison. Day after day you walk around and around, grinding grain for the evil Philistines.

A great holiday is approaching. It is a celebration of the fish-god, Dagon. The Philistines decide to bring you to Dagon's temple to make fun of you. They don't notice how much your hair has been growing during your months in prison.

At the temple, you hear the jeers and screams of the celebrating people. "I am tired," you tell the lad who is leading you around. "Let me lean against the big pillars that hold up the building. I need to rest."

He snickers at your weakness but places your left hand on one pillar and your right hand on another. "There, Samson, you rest here in the middle of the temple where everyone can see what a pitiful sight you are." He laughs as you bow your head. Your new long hair falls around your face as you pray.

Turn to page 116

Your stone flies sure and swift, smack into the middle of Goliath's great forehead. Goliath staggers, then falls with a mighty crash! You rush forward, pick up the giant's sword, and use it to cut Goliath's head from his body.

The Philistines, seeing the power of your God, turn and begin running. The soldiers of King Saul's army chase after them. While they are fighting, you reach down and grab up Goliath's huge head. You will take it to King Saul.

"Hey, watch it," a voice says. You look around and find that you are sitting in your Sunday school class. You have your hands around your friend Chuck's arm.

"Oh, I'm sorry," you mumble.

Your teacher is talking. "And so that is how David defeated Goliath." The teacher looks right at you. "I wonder how David must have felt that day. I guess we'll never know."

You smile and nod. Maybe no one else knows, but you have a pretty good idea how he must have felt. You know that with God's help, you could be exactly like David.

The End

Peter leads you to a place outside the walls of a city called Jerusalem. "This is the Place of the Skull. It is where Jesus was crucified. We Hebrews calls this place Golgotha."

"Golgotha?" you ask in a confused voice. "I always thought Jesus' cross was at a place called Calvary."

"Oh," Peter answers you, "that's the Roman word for the Place of the Skull."

You think a moment. "Place of the Skull, Golgotha, Calvary—they are different words, in different languages, for the same place, right?"

"Yes," Peter answers, "but what happened here is much more important than what word you choose to describe it. Jesus may have died that day, but He rose again. That is what matters. Would you like to see His empty tomb?" What do you answer?

If you want to see Jesus' empty tomb, turn to page 74
If you do not want to see Jesus' empty tomb, turn to page 107

"Well," Joseph begins, "God has revealed to me that you, my butler friend, will go to Pharaoh's house and be his butler."

The butler smiles broadly. Joseph asks a favor of him. "When you are in Pharaoh's house, would you tell him about me? I am unjustly imprisoned."

In a short while the butler is enjoying freedom and his job as Pharaoh's servant. But he doesn't mention Joseph.

Some time later the Pharaoh has a dream. He is troubled by it and calls all his wise men in to tell its meaning. None of them can help. Then the butler remembers Joseph and speaks to the Pharaoh.

"Once, my king, I had a dream while I was in your jail. My cellmate had one, too. A man there was able to tell us both what our dreams meant. I think he is still in prison."

"Send for him!" shouts Pharaoh to his guards.

"Come, Joseph," the head jailer calls. "The Pharaoh demands your presence!"

Should you ask to accompany Joseph, or stay where you are?

If you ask to go with Joseph, turn to page 81
If you stay in jail, turn to page 106

Elizabeth smiles as she tells you how, after years of asking, God sent them their very own child!

Zechariah explains that he did not believe it when an angel told him they were to have a child. He couldn't speak for months. He didn't get his voice back until the baby was eight days old and he went to the synagogue to name the child. "His name is John" were the first words Zechariah spoke.

You see the love these two have for the little one and you know his future must be very special. You thank these people for feeding you, sit back, close your eyes, and fall fast asleep. A sudden noise wakes you.

"What?" You look around and see you are sitting in your regular Sunday school class. "How did I— I mean—" You don't know what to say. The class giggles.

Your teacher begins talking. "We are studying the beginning of the book of Luke. Does anyone know what happens to Zechariah and Elizabeth?"

You smile and stand. "Yes. They are very, very old, but God lets them have a baby." You sit down, then add, "And they are very happy about it, too." Everyone laughs, and you join in.

The End

"Yes," you tell Peter. You walk with him to a small cave. Near the entrance is a huge stone.

"That was used to seal the tomb," Peter explains. "This place had been prepared for Joseph of Arimathea, but he gave it for a burial place for Jesus."

"How long was Jesus here?" you ask.

"Three days," Peter tells you. "Then, early one morning—he was gone. He rose from the dead." Peter shakes his head in wonder. "Pilate, the Roman governor, had soldiers on guard around the tomb. When an angel came and rolled the stone away, they fainted."

"Where is Jesus now?" you ask.

"He has returned to His father in heaven," Peter tells you. "But before He left, He promised to return someday. I spend my time traveling and telling all who will listen about Jesus and His teachings."

"Where will you go, now?"

"I'm on my way to the city of Lydda, near the Mediterranean Sea. Would you like to come along?"

You answer on page 107

Your stone flies sure and swift, smack into the heavy armor covering the giant's mammoth chest. Goliath roars with laughter and draws his huge sword. He swings it back and forth as he takes giant steps toward you. You hold tight to your slingshot and pouch of stones.

"Watch it," a voice says.

You look around and find that you are sitting in your Sunday school class, holding tight to your friend Chuck's arm.

Your teacher is talking. "And so, that is how David defeated Goliath with a stone to his—"

"I know," you say, waving your hand in the air. Your teacher nods and you explain. "I—David, I mean, had to hit the giant in the forehead. Otherwise his stone would have bounced off Goliath's heavy armor."

"I wonder how David must have felt that day," your teacher says. "I guess we'll never know."

You smile. You have a pretty good idea how he must have felt. You know that with God to help, you could be exactly like David.

The End

You stand at the door with Naaman and wait for Elisha. When nothing happens, you reach out and knock on the door. The door jerks open, and Elisha stands there.

"Why did you knock?" he asks. "You don't have to knock to come in."

"We don't?"

"We?"

"My friend N—," you turn to Naaman, but no one is there. "Well, he was here. Naaman has leprosy—"

"Leprosy? Oh, I remember, from our lesson last week," says your Sunday school teacher. Your teacher stands in the doorway of your classroom. "Come in, I'm glad you've been thinking about that story. Naaman was sure surprised when Elisha's servant met him at the door and told him to bathe seven times in the river, wasn't he?"

"We sure were," you answer. You take your seat and decide to read the story of Naaman and Elisha as soon as you get home today.

The End

Gehazi takes a bag of silver and several changes
of clothes from Naaman. You go along to see what
he does with them. Instead of going to Elisha's
house, he hides them in an old building. You ask
what he is doing.

Gehazi explains himself. "Naaman has lots of
money. He is a stranger to our land. It is not fair
that he should get off for free. I only took some of
what he had. He can easily spare it."

The man looks carefully at you. "If you keep my
secret, I will share with you." He holds up some
really nice clothes. Then he offers you some of his
silver.

You are tempted to accept some of Gehazi's
treasure. After all, you haven't done anything
wrong. What do you do?

If you accept Gehazi's offer, turn to page 109
If you refuse Gehazi's offer, turn to page 83

"Please," you ask the head jailer, "let me go with Joseph."

The man consults his records and looks sternly at you. "Well, young man, you came into this place with Joseph, I guess you might as well leave with him. Get going."

"Thanks," you call as you scramble to catch up with Joseph. You find him near the Pharaoh's throne.

"Are you the one who interprets dreams?" demands Pharaoh.

"It is not me. But my God can," Joseph answers. "He revealed to me the dream of a baker in the jail who was hung. He also revealed the meaning of your butler's dream—that he would work for you."

Pharaoh thinks all this over for a moment, then tells Joseph, "I want you to tell me about my dreams. I had two different dreams in one night. One dream had cattle in it. The other dream had grain in it."

You wonder about these two dreams. Which do you most want to hear Pharaoh describe?

If you choose the dream about cows, turn to page 85
If you choose the dream about grain, turn to page 86

This is so silly. You agree with Naaman that bathing in a river can't cure him. Naaman begins to moan over his pitiful condition, without even checking his skin.

But you have problems, too. You watch as your arms begin turning white with leprosy. Your fingers seem to be stuck together with a sticky goo. You dash toward the river and the possibility of a cure, but Naaman grabs you and holds you back.

"Certainly you don't believe—"

"Let me go. I must try, I must—" You struggle to reach the water.

"Relax. Don't be in such a rush," your Sunday school teacher tells you. He is holding onto you as you struggle.

"Ah—what—" You see that you are by the door of your Sunday school classroom.

"You were in an awful rush," your teacher says as he lets go of you. "Were you so anxious for our lesson?"

You look at your arms. They are healthy looking, no leprosy. You see jelly on your fingers from this morning's toast. Next time you will not be so quick to doubt Elisha.

The End

You tell Gehazi that you wouldn't feel right accepting any of the treasure that Elisha refused. He thinks you are crazy. When Gehazi has all his things hidden, you return with him to Elisha's house. The prophet is waiting for him.

"Where have you been?" Elisha asks.

"I didn't go anywhere," Gehazi answers him.

"Oh, Gehazi, you should not have taken the man's payment. Because you did, Naaman's leprosy shall come to you."

"Oh, no," says Gehazi. As you watch, great patches of his skin begin turning white. Soon the man is nearly covered with leprosy.

You are very impressed with the powers God has given the prophet.

"Let's go for a walk," Elisha tells you. After a short while the road divides. One way heads toward a place called Bethel. The other way points back to the Jordan River.

"We can go whichever way you choose," Elisha tells you. Which way do you pick?

If you pick the way to Bethel, turn to page 87
If you pick the way to the Jordan River, turn to page 88

Ananias steps back from you in fright. "You want me to baptize you? Then take you to my friends? This is a trick, and it won't work! I will not do it!"

"Ananias," you explain, "I met Jesus on the road—"

"Ha! You try to trick me! Jesus has gone—"

"A light and a voice came from heaven—that's how I became blind. Jesus Himself spoke to me."

But Ananias does not trust you and leaves. You have your sight, but what you want the most seems impossible to obtain.

"Why are you so sad?"

You turn and look into the face of your Sunday school teacher.

"I was just thinking about—does the Bible say anything about a man named Ananias restoring a man's eyesight?"

"Sure. He came to Saul when he had been struck down outside of Damascus. Then he and his friends taught Saul—or perhaps you remember him as Paul the missionary—all they knew about Jesus."

"They did? Oh, I'm so glad!" You smile and go on into your room. Your teacher just shakes his head and follows.

The End

"One dream," begins the Pharaoh, "started with me standing by the side of a stream. As I stood there, seven fat, healthy cows came up out of the water."

Your eyes grow wide in amazement at this story.

"What happened next?" Joseph asks.

Pharaoh goes on. "Seven more cows came up out of the stream. These were skinny and scraggly looking."

You wonder at this strange dream. "What did the cows do?" you ask.

"That is the part of the dream that has been troubling me. The seven skinny cows *ate* the seven fat cows—only they stayed skinny. They didn't look the least bit filled out."

You turn to Joseph. "What does it mean?"

"Silence!" shouts the Pharaoh. "I had the dreams, let him tell me the interpretation!"

"Well," says Joseph—

Turn to page 96

"One dream," begins the Pharaoh, "started when a stalk grew up before my eyes. It sprouted seven heads of grain. They were all filled out and had good heads."

Your eyes grow wide in amazement at this story.

"What happened next?" Joseph asks.

"Then," Pharaoh goes on, "another stalk grew up. It, too, sprouted seven heads of grain. These were all thin and withered."

You wonder at this strange dream. "What did the stalks do?" you ask.

"That is the part of the dream that has been troubling me. The seven thin heads of grain *ate* the seven good heads—only they stayed thin and withered. They didn't become fatter at all."

You turn to Joseph. "What does it mean?"

"Silence!" shouts the Pharaoh. "I had the dream, let him tell me the interpretation!"

"Well," says Joseph—

Turn to page 96

Elisha and you walk along a dusty road, and he begins telling you about the miracles God has worked through him, and about another prophet named Elijah. The discussion is interrupted by a large group of children from the nearby city. They see Elisha's bald head shining in the sun and begin teasing and mocking him.

"Look at his funny head," shouts one child.

"Elisha has a bald head, a bald head," sing the children.

Elisha, a prophet and spokesman for the God of all Israel, turns in anger and looks sternly at the children. He calls down a curse from God onto them. Then he continues on his way.

What do you want to happen to the mocking children?

If you want bears to come and attack them, turn to page 90
If you want the earth to open and swallow them, turn to page 93

88

You and the prophet of God, Elisha, walk along the Jordan River. Some friends of the prophet are working along the river bank.

"What are they doing?" you ask.

"They are building houses for themselves," Elisha tells you.

You decide to help. It is hard work, cutting down trees and lifting the big logs into place. You rest a bit and watch a man who is chopping down a tree.

Thwack! Thwack! His ax bites into the wood. Clunk! Splash! "Oh, no," the man cries, "the head flew off the ax and is lost!"

"It went into the river," you tell him. The two of you stand at the edge of the flowing water.

"What will I do? The ax belongs to my friend. I borrowed it for this work. How will I tell my friend I have lost his ax?"

Elisha hears the two of you talking and comes over to the edge of the river. But what can Elisha possibly do about a lost ax head?

If you think he can help, turn to page 94
If you think he cannot help, turn to page 103

Elisha turns from the unruly children and continues his walk. At the top of a hill you look back when you hear the sound of screams, miss your footing, and land on your left elbow. As you sit up and rub it, you look down below.

You see two large bears come charging out of the woods. One of the bears picks up a chanting child and throws it across the grass, then grabs another.

The second bear attacks a group of naughty children standing in a circle. Soon, broken and hurt children are lying all over the field. Then the bears roar loudly and lumber off into the woods.

From your lookout, high up on the hill, you count forty-two little bodies lying on the grass. You are very impressed with the power of Elisha's God.

You look ahead and see Elisha still walking down the road. Do you want to hurry and catch up with him, or sit and rest a while?

If you hurry after Elisha, turn to page 95
If you sit and rest a while, turn to page 113

Ananias and his friends rejoice that you now follow Jesus. They do everything they can to help you. When you thought the followers of Jesus were wrong, you pursued them with all your might. Now, you put the same energy into preaching for Jesus.

You go to the synagogue at Damascus and stand before the worshipers. "People of Damascus, I come to tell you about Jesus. He is the Son of God—"

"Blasphemer!"

"Shut him up!"

"Get him out of here!"

Some people believe you, but many want to kill you. One night a friend comes to you with a message.

"The people who hate you are waiting by the city gates. They intend to kill you when you go out in the morning."

Another friend has an idea. "Come, I know a way for you to escape."

You hesitate to run. It is so undignified! What do you decide to do?

If you confront the people at the gate, turn to page 102
If you go with your friend who knows a way out, turn to page 97

Elisha turns from the unruly children and continues his walk. At the top of a hill, you look back at the sound of screams. You can hardly wait to see the earth open up and swallow these nasty children.

Suddenly, the ground begins to shake under your feet. A great crack opens up, and you begin to fall.

"Elisha! Elisha!" you call out.

"That's right," your Sunday school teacher says.

You look around. You are sitting in your Sunday school classroom.

"You picked the right answer. Elisha was the Old Testament prophet who was mocked by the children. Then they were attacked by two large she-bears.

"Does anyone remember why the children were teasing Elisha?"

Everyone else shakes their head no, and so your teacher looks at you.

"Because of his bald head," you tell them.

"You must have really studied your Bible this week," your teacher comments.

"Well," you say, "something like that." Then you sit back and brush some strange-looking dust from your clothes.

The End

Elisha looks at the flowing water of the Jordan River. "Where did the ax head fall?" he asks.

"Somewhere right along here," you answer.

Elisha turns and walks to a scruffy-looking bush. He cuts off a stick and comes back to the bank of the river.

"Watch," he tells the two of you. Elisha flings the stick out into the water. It lands with a splash.

Then a strange thing happens. The man who was using the ax notices it first. "The iron ax head—it is floating! I can see my friend's ax." The happy man wades into the water and gets the ax head.

"Thank you, Elisha," he says, and goes away to put it back onto the handle.

"Elisha," you begin, "how can iron float? I saw it, but I can hardly believe it. How did you do it?"

Elisha explains on page 98

You hurry to catch up with Elisha. He is so far ahead you can hardly see him. You think of the bears that came out of the woods after the nasty, mocking children. This makes you afraid. You expect to see a bear come charging out from behind each tree you pass.

Elisha disappears from view as the path ahead goes around a bend. You run as fast as you can. A tree root has made a hump in the path, and you trip and fall. You land hard, on your left elbow, just as before. It really hurts now, but you get up and keep going. Where is Elisha?

Finally you see him just ahead and put on an extra burst of speed. You catch up and then have to decide what to do.

If you walk with Elisha along the Jordan River, turn to page 88
If you stop, rest, and rub your sore elbow, turn to page 113

You stand beside Joseph as he talks to the Pharaoh of Egypt. "Well," he begins, "your dreams tell about seven years of great plenty throughout the land of Egypt."

"Very good," smiles Pharaoh. "I like that."

"But," continues Joseph, "they will be followed by seven years of great famine."

"Oh, no," Pharaoh complains. "I must do something to change this."

"There is nothing you can do," Joseph tells him. "You had two dreams. One of cows and one of grain. This doubling of dreams means it cannot be changed!"

Pharaoh is very sad.

Joseph offers a suggestion to Pharaoh. "You could, sir, appoint officers over the land. They could save part of the harvest in each of the good years. Then there would be food left for the bad years."

You start to tell Joseph what a good idea you think this is, but Pharaoh speaks first. As he talks, you accept a dried fig from a dish his servant is passing around.

"Good idea. Now who I will choose to head up this important project?" Who does Pharaoh choose?

If he chooses his chief ambassador, turn to page 101
If he chooses you, turn to page 104
If he chooses Joseph, turn to page 105

You decide to slip away. Your friend takes you through the winding streets of Damascus.

"Where are we going?" you ask.

"To a place where you can escape from this city. Too many people here have heard you preach about Jesus. They think you have dangerous ideas and want to kill you. Perhaps you can return in a few years."

"I must tell them—"

"I know, but you can't do much preaching if you are dead, can you?" You turn a corner, and your friend shows you a narrow set of steps leading to a second-floor apartment. "Up there, hurry. Other friends are waiting at the top."

You climb the stairs, and someone grabs your arm. "Here, get into this basket."

"*Me?* In a basket like a chicken going to market? Do you think I—"

"Shhhhhh, they will hear you. Get inside and be very quiet." Your friends stuff you into a big basket and take it to a window of the apartment. What will they do next?

Find out on page 99

98

Elisha looks sternly at you. "Have you not learned anything? By now you should know the answer to that question." Elisha walks off and leaves you to ponder the miracle of the floating ax head. You pull some leaves from a bush and crumple them in your fingers as you think. Then you realize your mistake.

"Elisha didn't make the ax head float! He just let God use him by tossing in the stick!" you exclaim.

"Very good reasoning," your Sunday school teacher says.

"What?" You look around and see that you are in your Sunday school classroom. How did you get *here*? The last thing you remember—

"Yes," your teacher continues, "Elisha was used by God many times."

You sit back and decide you must have been dreaming. Then you notice you have a bunch of crumpled leaves in your hand. Now you really wonder!

The End

Your friends' apartment is one of those built into the wide walls surrounding the city of Damascus. They struggle to get the basket you are stuffed into up on the windowsill. Someone ties a stout rope around it. Then they work to push your basket through the narrow window. All of a sudden, the basket pops through and you are suspended in the air, outside the walls of the city.

This is scary! You hold tight as the basket sways and spins around. You try hard not to get dizzy. The basket finally hits the ground with a thump, and you carefully open your eyes.

Your eyes open to see—your Sunday school teacher standing at the front of the class talking. How can this be? You were—

"And, class," your teacher continues, "that's how Paul escaped from Damascus."

"He was awfully dizzy in that basket," you offer.

"Well," your teacher smiles, "he might have been. I guess we can't know for sure."

You sit back and remember. Maybe no one else is sure, but you are!

The End

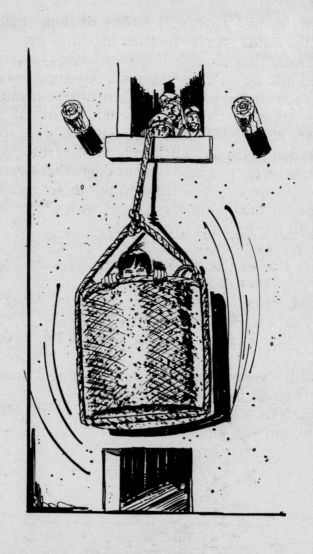

"You, Chief Ambassador," Pharaoh orders.

"The chief ambassador?" you say.

"Not again! Have you been daydreaming in class again?"

You stare at your Sunday school teacher, who is standing right in front of you. "Not me. I always pay attention," your voice says. Your head trys to figure out how you ended up here.

"If you have been paying such close attention to our lesson, why don't you tell us who Pharaoh chose to head his grain-saving project?"

"Well," you consider, "I don't think it was the chief ambassador or me." The entire class breaks up with laughter. Your teacher's face turns a deep shade of red.

Quickly, you add, "Joseph! Because God revealed Pharaoh's dreams to him—the dreams about the cattle and the grain and—"

"Okay," your teacher cuts in. "I'm impressed. For once you seem to know what's going on."

You sit back and notice a dried fig in your hand—how? No, no one would *ever* believe! You pop the fig into your mouth and smile.

The End

"No," you tell your friends, "I will wait until morning and go out the city gate. I have too much pride to run away!"

Early the next morning you stride confidently through the city gate. "There he is! Get him! Kill him!" shout a group of men. Rocks start to fly. One hits you on the knee, and your leg buckles under you.

"Stop!" you yell. "I only want to explain—" Your words are cut off by a well-aimed stone to your face. "Ouch!"

"Oh, I'm sorry."

Your hand goes up to your sore cheek. "I'm really sorry," says your best friend, Chuck. "I didn't mean to bump you. I tripped and my elbow sort of flew out."

You see you are standing outside your Sunday school classroom. "How did I get here?" you begin.

"What?" Chuck asks.

"Never mind." You slip into your classroom and listen to your teacher tell how Paul escaped from Damascus over a wall in a basket. Good for him, you think. He would have had real problems if he had been too proud to listen to his friends.

The End

You don't think even Elisha can find a small iron ax head in the rushing waters of the Jordan River!

As you watch, Elisha cuts a stick from a bush and tosses it into the water. Some water splashes on your arm, and you wipe at it. Silly Elisha, you think. Then you remember Naaman, his leprosy, and what happened to Gehazi. You look again at the water splashed on your arm.

"I'm sorry," says Chuck.

You look up and see your best friend, Chuck, standing by the drinking fountain outside your Sunday school room.

Chuck tries again. "I'm sorry I splashed you. Something is wrong with this fountain." He demonstrates by stepping on the pedal again with a smile. Water shoots in a high arc and splashes onto your arm. You jump back.

"Okay, boys, stop fooling around and get to class," your Sunday school teacher says. "Our lesson this week is about Elisha and how he saves an ax head for his friend." You hurry to class. You can hardly wait to find out how he locates the ax.

The End

"You!" orders Pharaoh, pointing right at you!

"*Me?* Do you mean me?"

"Of course I mean you. What's the matter? Have you been daydreaming in class again?"

You stare at your Sunday school teacher, who is standing right in front of you. "Not me. I always pay attention," your voice says. Your head trys to figure out how you ended up here.

"If you have been paying such close attention to our lesson, why don't you tell us who Pharaoh chose to head his grain saving project?"

"Well," you consider, "I don't think it was me." The entire class breaks up with laughter. Your teacher's face turns a deep shade of red.

Quickly, you add, "Joseph! Because God revealed Pharaoh's dreams to him—the dreams about the cattle and the grain and—"

"Okay," your teacher cuts in, "I'm impressed. For once you seem to know what's going on."

You sit back and notice a dried fig in your hand—how? No, no one would *ever* believe. You pop the fig into your mouth and smile.

The End

"Joseph!" orders Pharaoh. "God revealed the dreams to him; perhaps God will help him with this project."

"Joseph!" you repeat. How great for your friend.

"Joseph? That's right. And I thought you had been daydreaming in class again!"

You stare at your Sunday school teacher, standing right in front of you. "Not me. I always pay attention," your voice says. Your head trys to figure out how you ended up here.

"Since you have been paying such close attention to our lesson, why don't you tell us why Pharaoh chose Joseph to head up his grain saving project?"

"Because he told Pharaoh about the cows and grain in his dreams." You hesitate, and then go on, "And the dreams of the people in jail, the baker and the butler—"

"Okay," your teacher cuts in. "For once you seem to know what's going on."

You sit back and notice a dried fig in your hand—how? No, no one would *ever* believe it. You pop the fig into your mouth and smile.

The End

You decide to stay in the jail. After a long time you hear that Joseph is becoming a very important person. You decide to try to escape and get to him.

One night you manage to sneak past the jailer and begin to run. The jailer chases you. You run and run. He is gaining on you, so you try harder, but a hand closes over your shoulder.

"No running in the halls."

You look up into the face of your Sunday school teacher. You are standing, breathless, outside your classroom.

"Oh," you begin, "I'm sorry. You see—"

"Hi," interrupts your best friend. "Will you tell us the rest of the story you started last week?" he says to your teacher. "Remember, Joseph was getting ready to interpret some dreams."

"Not Joseph," you correct him. They both look at you. "Only God interprets dreams. Joseph only told what God revealed to him. He told me—well, I mean—that's the way it was."

Your teacher begins telling the story to the class, and you sit back and wish you had stayed with Joseph a while longer.

The End

"No, I have got to be going. I'm kind of lost, you see. It's hard to explain."

"Why don't you try looking on the other side of those bushes," Peter suggests with a smile. Then he strides off.

You shrug and push your way through the thick brush Peter indicated. You trip, lose your balance, and sit down very hard, bumping the arm of a boy about your own age.

"Watch it," your best friend, Chuck, says.

"Boys," says your Sunday school teacher, "you are supposed to be looking up the meaning of the word 'Golgotha.' "

"I know that!" you answer. "My friend Peter explained it. Golgotha means 'Place of the Skull'. In Latin, the language of the Romans, the word is 'Calvary'."

"Your friend Peter sounds like he knows a lot about Bible times. Perhaps you could bring him to class sometime," suggests your teacher.

"Aaaaaaaaah, well, I'm not sure that would be possible," you say.

"You could ask him," your teacher says.

"Sure," you answer. "The next time I see him." You sit back with a sigh of relief and wonder if you will see your friend Peter again.

The End

You are sure Zechariah and Elizabeth are too old to have a young child of their own. You know they must have found him.

Elizabeth tries to explain that John is really theirs, but you start to laugh at the idea of these two old people and the tiny child. You laugh and laugh.

"Why are you laughing?" your Sunday school teacher asks.

"What?" You look around. You are sitting in your Sunday school class.

"How did I—I mean—" You don't know what to say. The class laughs.

Your teacher begins talking. "We are studying the book of Luke. Do you know what happens to Zechariah and Elizabeth?"

You grin and stand. "Yes. They are very, very old. But God lets them have a baby of their own." You sit down, then add, "And they are very happy about it, too." Everyone laughs, and you join in.

"Yes, I'm sure they were," your teacher agrees.

As the lesson continues you sit back and smile. You know exactly how glad John's parents were—really!

The End

You tell Gehazi that you really appreciate his sharing with you, and put on some of the new clothes. You tuck away a handful of silver. Then the two of you return to Elisha's house. The prophet is waiting.

"Where have you been?" Elisha asks.

"I didn't go anywhere," Gehazi answers him.

"Oh, Gehazi, you should not have taken the man's payment. Because you did, Naaman's leprosy will come to you."

"Oh no!" says Gehazi. As you watch, great patches of his skin begin turning white. Soon the man is nearly covered with leprosy.

You look down and see blotches forming on your arms, too.

"No! No!" you yell.

"What's the matter?" your Sunday school teacher asks.

You look up and find yourself standing in the hall outside your classroom. You look at both of your arms. They are normal and healthy. What a close call! You go on into your classroom, thinking about what life must have been like for poor, greedy Gehazi.

The End

You have enough problems without trying to argue with your owners. Joseph is taken off to jail and you stay behind in Potiphar's house. Things are not too bad for a while. Sometimes you wonder about Joseph. Then Potiphar's wife decides that she does not like you any more. She talks her husband into selling you in the slave market.

"No! Not back to the slave market," you plead. You try to get away, but trip and hit your head. Everything goes black.

"Lie still, you'll feel better soon."

"Oh, please don't sell me. No! No!"

"What's wrong with my son?" your father asks. You try to tell him about Potiphar's wife, but the words get all jumbled.

"He was running in the hall and tripped and hit his head," your Sunday school teacher tells your dad.

"I don't know what happened to Joseph."

Your teacher smiles "You must not be hurt too bad if you are worried about missing your Sunday school lesson."

No one understands. You wonder if you will ever find out what happened to your friend Joseph.

The End

You think what a silly thing this vow of a Nazirite is and laugh. Once you start laughing, it is hard to stop.

"Stop that," your Sunday school teacher asks. "Samson's pledge was a holy vow to God. It wasn't silly. It was an outward sign of his relationship with God."

You stop laughing rather suddenly, as you find yourself sitting in your Sunday school classroom. This is confusing!

Your teacher continues with the lesson. "God gave Samson his great strength so that he could help his people."

"I wish I had a chance to be that strong. I'd do anything God wanted!" one of the other boys says.

"Well," your teacher continues, "Samson wasn't perfect, but before his life ended he did a lot of great things."

"Don't you wish you could have a chance to do something like that?" your friend asks you.

You remember how you felt when the lion attacked and you suddenly had such strength. Your friend doesn't know how much you wish you hadn't laughed.

The End

112

"Jesus is the Son of God. That's what I believe—just like Stephen," you add defiantly. Several of the men standing around begin coming closer. A couple of them reach for stones. You reach down and pick up a rock to throw back. You take one step backward, then another, and bump into someone, hard.

"Watch it," exclaims Chuck, your best friend.

"Boy, am I glad to see you! Those—" You turn around and all the men are gone. Instead, you see your friends going into their Sunday school rooms.

"Let's get to class," Chuck suggests.

"Okay, sure," you answer, still puzzled by what has happened. What a crazy daydream!

"Our lesson," your Sunday school teacher begins, "is about Stephen and how he was stoned for his beliefs."

"That seems kind of extreme," Chuck exclaims.

"But," you volunteer, "that's what happened. The people used real stones"—you notice your hand is still closed over a rock—real stones, just like this!" And you hold up the stone for everyone to see.

The End

You decide to sit down, rub your sore elbow, and rest for a while. So many strange and exciting things have been happening that you are exhausted. Just a few minutes' sleep and maybe you'll try to catch up with Elisha.

You open your eyes with a jerk and wonder how long you have been sleeping. You look at your watch. Sunday school is almost over! Sunday school? Now you notice you are sitting in the hall near your Sunday school room.

"Oh, no!" you exclaim. It must have all been a dream. And it seemed so real—Elisha's shiny bald head, Naaman's leprosy, your sore elbow—it is hard to believe you only dreamed them.

You start to get up, and feel your left elbow. It is very sore. You look and see that you have scraped it somehow. You wonder—could you really have been with Elisha?

The End

You run your fingers through the soft, fuzzy wool of the lamb and tell it about your bravery.

"I am fearless! Nothing can hurt me. I am so great that—"

Just then you hear a loud roar. Looking up, you see the lion coming to its feet. *Oh, no!* You reach out, but it is too late. The lion springs. You fall backward under its great weight. "Aaaaaaah!"

"Hey, you're blocking the way," someone says.

"What do you mean?" you answer, looking around. You find yourself outside your Sunday school room. You reach down to touch the soft lamb again. You only feel your jelly-sticky hand.

"You're almost late. Where have you been?" one of your classmates asks.

You shrug and go into your class. No one would ever believe where you had been.

The End

You are just too sleepy to get up. You roll over and pull the pillow over your head. Soon you are fast asleep. You don't hear your family leave for church. You don't hear your dog barking or the birds chirping. You sleep on and on.

"O God, strengthen me," you pray. "Lord, let me punish the Philistines."

God hears your prayer, and you feel your arms fill with His power. You push against the two pillars. They collapse with a great roar. Other pillars give way under the sudden strain. Soon the whole temple comes crashing down. Many Philistines are crushed. Giant stone blocks fall on you, too.

"Aaaaah!"

"Well," your Sunday school teacher says, "don't get upset. The Scriptures tell us Samson died that day when he avenged the horrible things the Philistines had done to him."

You look around and see that you are sitting in your Sunday school class. How did you get here? You can feel Samson's pain and frustration as if it were your own. You shake your head and wonder. You must have dreamed it all.

As your teacher goes on with the story, you rub at your eyes. They feel sore and strange. You couldn't really have—or could you?

The End

Plop! You land on the hot ground. You get a mouthful of sand. By the time you get enough of it out of your mouth to yell, everyone is gone.

You sit up and look around. Only sand. In every direction all you can see is sand. It is so hot! It is hard to get up, because your hands are still tied. You walk a while and fall again.

"Aaaaaaaaawww! Aaaaaww!" A large bird circles about you, but you are too thirsty and tired to get up and go on.

"Aw, come on, you're blocking the steps."

Your eyes jolt open, and you find yourself in the hall near your Sunday school classroom.

"Let's go," someone calls. "Church is over."

When you pass the drinking fountain you stop for a long, cool drink. In the car, your dad asks you what your lesson was about.

"Well," you begin, "there were some sheep, then a lion, and they put me on a camel and—"

Your dad just shakes his head and drives home. You quietly brush sand from your clothes.

The End

You hurry away before you get into more trouble. You leave the road and push your way into some thick bushes to hide. You stumble forward and bump into Chuck, your best friend.

"Chuck, what are you doing here?"

"Oh," Chuck answers you with a grin, "I come here all the time."

You look around and see that you are in the hall just outside your Sunday school room. You follow your friend into the room and sit down, feeling very confused.

"Our lesson," your Sunday school teacher begins, "is about Stephen and how he was stoned for his beliefs."

Chuck leans over and whispers to you, "I bet those stones could really hurt."

You rub a purple bruise on your arm and whisper back, "I think you are absolutely right!"

The End

"No, I have to be going. I'm kind of lost, you see. It's hard to explain."

"Why don't you try looking on the other side of those bushes?" Peter suggests with a smile. Then he strides off.

You push your way through the thick brush, trip, lose your balance, and sit down very hard.

"Watch it," your best friend, Chuck, says.

"Boys," says your Sunday school teacher. "You are supposed to be looking up Peter's reactions to Jesus' being arrested."

"I know that! My friend Peter said he didn't know Jesus, three different times. Peter was so sad and sorry. But Peter really loved Jesus. Sometimes it's awfully hard to admit being a believer. People may even throw stones at you, like happened to that guy Stephen."

"Yes," your Sunday school teacher agrees. "It's a lot easier to be brave sitting here safe in class than at school or on the playground."

You rub the bruise on your arm and nod your head. But, you think, like Peter, that you will do better next time.

The End

If you would like to read more about the people you have met in this book, check below for where to step into YOUR BIBLE and find them.